EDITED BY HELEN EXLEY
ILLUSTRATED BY JULIETTE CLARKE

Published simultaneously in 1998 by Exley Publications in Great Britain, and Exley Publications LLC in the USA.
Copyright © Helen Exley 1998
The moral right of the author has been asserted.

12 11 10 9 8 7 6 5 4 3 2 1

ISBN 1-86187-118-X

A copy of the CIP data is available from the British Library. All rights reserved. No part of this publication may be reproduced in any form. Printed in China.
Exley Publications Ltd, 16 Chalk Hill, Watford, Herts WD1 4BN, UK.
Exley Publications LLC, 232 Madison Avenue, Suite 1206, NY 10016, USA.
To Momtom

The publishers are grateful for permission to reproduce copyright material. Whilst every reasonable effort has been made to trace copyright holders, the publishers would be pleased to hear from any not here acknowledged. IAIN CRICHTON-SMITH: From "The Chair in Which You've Sat" from Love Poems and Elegies, published by Victor Gollancz, an imprint of Cassell. KATHERINE BUTLER HATHAWAY: From "The Journals and Letters of the Little Locksmith". LIZ SMITH: from "The Mother Book", published by Granada, an imprint of HarperCollins Publishers Ltd. HARRIET WALTER: From "Still Working On It" from "Mothers by Daughters", edited by Joanna Goldsworthy. Published by Virago Press Ltd. © 1995 Harriet Walter.

A LITTLE BOOK FOR MY

Mother

A HELEN EXLEY GIFTBOOK

EXLEY
NEW YORK • WATFORD, UK

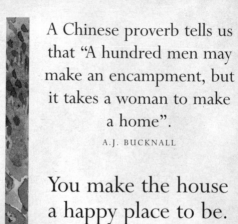

A Chinese proverb tells us that "A hundred men may make an encampment, but it takes a woman to make a home".

A.J. BUCKNALL

You make the house a happy place to be.

SIAN FITZPATRICK, AGE 8

Mothers applaud absolutely
anything worthy of praise.
A button done up alone.
A new word.
A head-over-heels.
And the child smiles —
and soars a little higher.

PAM BROWN, b.1928

In the eyes of its mother, every beetle is a gazelle.

MOROCCAN
PROVERB

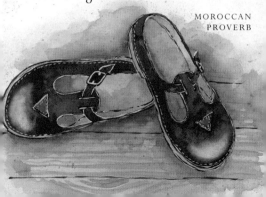

She is the one they can count on for the things that matter most of all. She is their food and their bed and their extra blanket when it grows cold in the night; she is their warmth and health and their shelter; she is the one they want to be near when they cry.

KATHERINE BUTLER HATHAWAY

A mother is a person
who seeing there are
only four pieces of pie
for five people,
promptly announces she
never did care for pie.

TENNEVA JORDAN

All mothers are rich when they love their children. There are no poor mothers, no ugly ones, no old ones. Their love is always the most beautiful of the joys.

MAURICE MAETERLINCK

Do you know I was born
because I wanted to be
near my mommy?

CLAUDIA MARTINEZ, AGE 8

HOME MADE
JAM FROM MOM
IS REALLY
BOTTLED LOVE.

H.M.E.

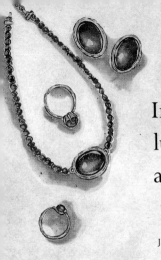

In a child's
lunch box,
a mother's
thoughts.

JAPANESE PROVERB

There is nobody I know like my mother. My mother is like the earth, full of goodness and strong. When I'm asleep my mother lights up the dark corners and gently wakes me up. When the day comes hot and stuffy, my mother cools me like the rain does.

SHAH RAHMAN, AGE 10½

Mothers have every intention of letting you go, letting you lead your own life, never interfering.
But they just can't help phoning to see if you have enough socks. And are eating properly.

PAM BROWN, b.1928

Dear Mother: I'm all right.
Stop worrying about me.

EGYPTIAN PAPYRUS LETTER,
c.2000 BC

worry, worry, worry

A mother has a built-in
worry mechanism —
without an off switch.

PAM BROWN, b.1928

A mother is someone to help you eat your food when you can't eat it all, so it looks like you ate it all.

TERI BURNS, AGE 11

My mum is a bit stupid because every time I ask for something she buys it me.

DEBBIE, AGE 10

I have a super mother who makes cakes, puts them in the pantry and doesn't notice when I eat them.

MARK WICKHAM-JONES, AGE 13

I have... learned to really hear the message my mother has given me all my life: "I will be with you always". As in forever, into the eternal hereafter, no matter what.

REBECCA WALKER,
DAUGHTER OF ALICE WALKER

My mother means morning.

A beautiful morning.

ABBY, AGE 7

I feel happy and bubbly

when Mummy laughs.

SUZANAH OCCARDI

She is kind and gentle.

Sometimes my mother

really loves me and she

looks at my face

and smiles at me.

I go and sit by her.

BALBINDER KAUR KALSI, AGE 11

*A mother has
the magic glue
that sticks
broken pieces
together.*

PAM BROWN, b.1928

A mother is a woman with a twenty-five hour day who can still find an hour to play with her family.

IRIS PECK

A mother is neither cocky, nor proud, because she knows the school principal may call at any minute to report that her child had just driven a motorcycle through the gymnasium.

MARY KAY BLAKELY, b.1957

*If I were my mother my children
would have to go to bed at ten
o'clock at night and get up at ten
in the morning too. They would be
sent to school once a week just to
keep up the good education.
When it was a birthday I would
not insist on inviting someone like
Celia Pigface to the party.*

KATY BERGER, AGE 11

A DEFINITION
I ONCE HEARD OF
A MOTHER IS
"SOMEONE WHO
HOPES FOR YOU".

FROM "THE FRIENDSHIP BOOK
OF FRANCIS GAY"

My mother is like a tall fruit tree because she is strong, tall and big. My mother is like morning because she is like sun shine coming up. My mother is like a mango because she is sweet and delicious. My mother is like the thunder because she is sometimes angry with me. My mother is like an armchair because she is cosy and warm.

TANIA TSIMABA BUEYA, AGE 8½

A mother's love means a life's devotion – and sometimes a life's sacrifice – with but one thought, one hope and one feeling, that her children will grow up healthy and strong, free from evil habits and able to provide for themselves.

AUTHOR UNKNOWN

MOTHERHOOD

Mothers have as powerful
an influence over
the welfare of future
generations as all other
earthly causes combined.

JOHN S.C. ABBOT

There shall never be
another quite so tender,
quite so kind as the
patient little mother;
nowhere on this earth
you'll find her affection
duplicated....

PAUL C. BROWNLOW

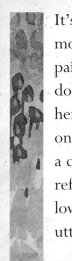

It's the three pairs of eyes that mothers have to have.... One pair that see through closed doors. Another in the back of her head... and, of course, the ones in front that can look at a child when he goofs up and reflect "I understand and I love you" without so much as uttering a word.

ERMA BOMBECK, b.1927

A mother understands what a child does not say.

JEWISH PROVERB

Anything that happens, you can confide in Mama. Mama loves each child the way God loves His children. Nothing's too bad to tell Mama. Don't ever tell me a lie. It's not necessary, because Mama will understand.

HONORE DE BALZAC (1799-1850)

*My mother is a lady who has
had a lot of problems in her life.
Most of them me....*

DIANA BRISCOE

God didn't have enough arms
for keeping kids out of trouble
so he invented moms.

ALICE LUMPKIN, AGE 11

When it is time for me to tidy
up my bedroom I hide things
under the bed. I don't know
how she knows they are there.

RACHEL DARBON, AGE 6, FROM EXLEY'S
"TO THE WORLD'S BEST MOTHER"

The most vivid
memories of my youth
are linked with my
mother's kitchen
coming home to the
warmth of a log fire and
good food, lovingly
prepared.

MARGARET FULTON

*It doesn't matter
how old I get, whenever
I see anything new
or splendid,
I want to call, "Mom,
come and look".*

HELEN EXLEY, b.1943

SHE'S IMPOSSIBLE!

My mother has weird rules that I have to obey, like having a bath, keeping my room tidy and even having my hair cut.

CHRISTOPHER MOATES, AGE 12

When the son leaves home his doting
mother gives him two cashmere sweaters
as going-away presents. Wanting to show
his appreciation, the boy comes home
for Thanksgiving wearing one of the
sweaters. The mother greets him at the
door. She takes a long, anxious look and
says: "What's the matter? The other
sweater you didn't like?"

LIZ SMITH, FROM "THE MOTHER BOOK"

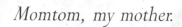

Momtom, my mother.

You're always there in my thoughts. You always will be there. Your gifts have not been <u>things</u>, although you always gave your most precious things too.

Your gifts have been your constancy, your laughter, your enthusiasm (especially your over-enthusiasm!), the very richness, the festivals, of life.

H.M.E.

... SOMETIMES ONE
NEEDS A QUIET
KITCHEN, A CUP OF
COFFEE AND ONE'S
MOTHER.

PAM BROWN, b.1928

Mothers remember everything you ever did or said — and tell your friends, in graphic detail.

PAM BROWN, b.1928

Never tell your kids how well you did at school. Mum still has your reports.

ITOKO FUJITA

The trouble with mothers
is that however well
groomed and sophisticated
you appear to strangers,
they know your knickers
are probably held up with a
safety pin.

SAMANTHA ARMSTRONG

A small child
glories in a mother
who has skills and
successes outside
the family.
So long as they
know that she
loves them better
than anything.

PAM BROWN, b.1928

One of my children wrote in a third-grade piece on how her mother spent her time... "one-half time on home, one-half time on outside things, one-half time writing."

CHARLOTTE MONTGOMERY

... when a child
needs a mother
to talk to, nobody
else but a mother
will do.

ERICA JONG,
b.1942,
FROM "FEAR OF FIFTY"

... an entire division of living
men has been used, during
wartime, or at any time,
to spell out the word "mom"
on a drill field.

PHILIP WYLIE

Inside every elderly human being
is a child missing its mother.

HELEN THOMSON

That dear octopus from whose
tentacles we never quite escape, nor
in our innermost hearts
never quite wish to.

DODIE SMITH (1896-1990)

A little child loves its
mother with all its heart and
soul and being – clings to
her touch, her words, her
certainty.
Trusts absolutely.
Knows with complete
conviction that it is the
centre of her world.

PAM BROWN, b.1928

The chair in which you've sat's
not just a chair
nor the table at which you've just
eaten just a table
nor the window that you've
looked from just a window.
All these have now a patina of
your body and mind....

IAIN CRICHTON SMITH

Any mother could perform the jobs of several air traffic controllers with ease.

LISA ALTHER, b. 1944

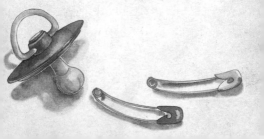

How did you manage
to reach degree standard
in such challenging subjects
as lullaby singing,
soap bubble blowing,
and the vanquishing of
nightmare bug-a-boos?

CHRISTINE HARRIS

The _warmest_

bed of all

is Mother's.

JEWISH PROVERB

The happiness that families share is the greatest joy in the world. The knowledge that there is always someone who cares is a treasure nothing can match. The love of a family makes life beautiful.

ANDREW HARDING ALLEN

A mother is the lady who, up to her eyes in the washing can be compiling a grocery list, explaining the causes of the Hundred Years War, mixing an authentic grass green from a worn-out paint box, finding a lost ballet shoe, rubbing down a saturated dog, watching a batch of cakes and dealing with a Jehovah's Witness.

PAM BROWN, b.1928

She is the person you can come to for comfort, when all hope is lost, like an old teddy bear with one eye and half an ear.

PATRICIA BOWIE, AGE 13

My mother is so kind I do not know how to thank her. How can I thank you my Mommy?

DAVID WEBB, AGE 9

When you are ill, who is
always there,
Quietly sitting stroking
your hair?
Who is always waiting for you to
come home?
Who welcomes you with open arms?
Who never lets you down?
Who wakes you up with a lovely
smile in the morning?
Who's always ready to help?

VIVIENNE GILBERT

If evolution really works,
how come mothers have
only two hands?

ED DUSSAULT

My mother gets up between six and half past am and she does some general housework and makes breakfast. At seven she wakes up my two brothers and they all have breakfast. Then Mammy gets the boys ready for school, wakes up Daddy, and at quarter to eight she goes off to work.

JOANNA BLAKE, AGE 11

Mothers need transfusions
fairly often —
phone calls, letters,
bright postcards from
the Outer Hebrides.

HEULWEN ROBERTS

Only a mother can
send hugs by post.

PAM BROWN, b.1928

To a mother
her middle-
aged child
is six going
on sixteen
in heavy
disguise.

PAM BROWN, b.1928

A mother's great ambition when you are grown is to find an excuse to tuck you up in bed and ply you with soup.

CHARLOTTE GRAY, b.1937

A mother packs strange "essentials" in your rucksack. Like chlorodyne and salt tablets, when you're only going fifty miles.

PAM BROWN, b.1928

*Your hands held mine
until I could walk alone.
You taught me freedom —
and when the time had
come you let me go.*

PAM BROWN, b.1928

She doesn't know how to cook
very well but when she cooks
the dinner it seems to have
something special about it.
When she makes my bed I
think she puts something into
it, and I don't awake all night.

CONCHITA REY BENAYAS, AGE 10

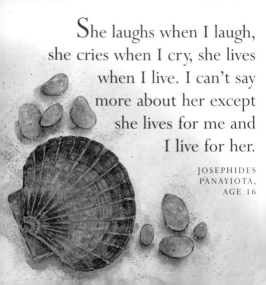

She laughs when I laugh,
she cries when I cry, she lives
when I live. I can't say
more about her except
she lives for me and
I live for her.

JOSEPHIDES
PANAYIOTA,
AGE 16

Whether you like it or not,
your mother goes with you.
Forever.

HELEN EXLEY, b.1943

She is soaked through everything
I see. I look at my face
in the mirror, at my mannerisms,
the veins in my hands and realise
she will always be with me.

HARRIET WALTER,
FROM "MOTHERS – BY DAUGHTERS"

A mother will drop everything,
cancel everything, beg or borrow
fares, sling a nightdress
in a bag and be with you
in a time that would make a
Record Breaker blink.
Whenever, wherever you
need her.

CHARLOTTE GRAY, b.1937

Thank you for being there
come fire, flood or penury.
Thank you for being ready
to lend anything,
give anything that will help
us through.

PAM BROWN, b.1928

A dribble of baby-food
on your dress,
a splodge of pastry-mix
in your hair....
These are the badges
awarded to all
lovely mothers.
Wear yours with pride.

CHRISTINE HARRIS

If a thing was worth seeing,
or hearing or smelling or
touching or testing –
you would get me there –
come hell or high water, come
mud, snow, rain or lack of
cash in hand. Thank you for
a life filled with memories
to see me through.

PAM BROWN, b.1928